BUILDING FINANCIAL MUSCLE

FOR ANYONE WHO WANTS TO LIVE WITHOUT FINANCIAL STRESS FOREVER

By Karen G

Author: Karen G

Title: Building Financial Muscle

Subtitle: For Anyone Who Wants to Live Without Financial Stress Forever

Subjects: Education; Financial Education; Money and Mindset Development; Money Management; Debt; Savings; Financial Planning; Financial Curriculum and Development; Marketing

Get Karen's FREE course: How To Build Financial Muscle
www.howtobuildfinancialmuscle.com

Join the Facebook group Official Karen G Community

See the back page of this book for your FREE ECOURSE

Contents

TESTIMONIALS

Karen has taught me a set of simple strategies to help manage my money.

I am now in control of my financial situation instead of it controlling me.

My life now looks totally different. I don't constantly worry about paying the next bill. Even though there have been some unexpected hiccups along the way, in twelve months I have paid down the majority of my debt and started saving whilst still having a life.

Thank you so much, Karen, for your guidance and understanding. I'm so grateful to you and would have never been able to do this without your help.

- Nikita Tsukaguchi

Karen has a unique quality and approach with regard to debt management and wealth creation.

She has successfully over the past 20 years; dealt with thousand of clients to put into effect a fast track system for financial freedom. You will have the bonus of her knowledge and expertise on tap combined with a proven measurable system that will keep you on track to achieve your financial freedom goals fast.

If you're looking to give yourself a financial promotion and be the boss of your future then Karen is the person to help you do just that.

- Harry Bozin

Karen is a wonderful coach and truly takes her task to heart. Her help and advice has certainly helped in shaping myself for the future. Keep up the great work please!

- Dave Pallett

INTRODUCTION

I often talk about building financial muscle in my work with clients, both through the programs I offer and on social media. And I do it all for a good reason.

Why? Because people today still don't have their money working for them, and they're making dumb decisions when it comes to managing it effectively.

When I was writing this book, our world experienced something we'd never seen before.

A pandemic of massive proportions.

It's was called COVID-19 (and still is at the time of this release) a deadly disease that killed hundreds of thousands of people around the world.

It started in China and soon spread across the globe. Most of us have never seen a disease expand and multiply like that before.

The world went into lockdown and jobs were lost.

Millions of people around the world have suffered not only physically with their health or emotionally from being isolated and confined to their homes, but also from being financially crippled due to a lack of work and money.

Sadly, the majority of people don't have any savings. They don't have between six and nine months of emergency money to save them while they're out of work and unable to put food on the table, keep the roof over their head or pay their bills.

We've been through many economic challenges, and I'm sure we're going to go through many more. But what we recently experienced (and are still experiencing with COVID-19) is impacting people as I've never seen before.

This has to be one of the most uncertain times people throughout the world have experienced—not just for their health but also for the drastic measures that have been put into place.

Currently we're being quarantined, countries are in lockdown and people have to stay in their own homes just to protect themselves from getting the virus. Our elderly in nursing care aren't able to see any visitors, which is detrimental not only to their physical health but to their mental health as well.

People are experiencing high levels of anxiety, panic and stress due to the financial pressure of being unable to work and being sent home on unpaid leave when their employers suffer significant financial loss.

When people have something behind them in the form of savings, some of this pressure is relieved. That's because they know that for the short period of time they're out of work, they have money to keep them afloat.

Building financial muscle is about providing security and protection when major events like COVID-19 occur.

One of my other concerns is retirement. When people decide around age 65 or 70 that they would like to retire, they're going to struggle financially again!

Why? Because when they come out of a crisis, some will go back to their old ways of mismanaging money.

So when they get to their retirement years, they'll have learnt nothing. Instead, they'll pick up where they left off before COVID-19 and spend everything they earn, leaving nothing for them to live on at the end of their working life.

Financial muscle, as I bang on about constantly, is making sure firstly that your hard-earned money is working for you and not for your bank.

And secondly, it's about having something put away for "just in case", because "just in case" comes up a fair bit during every lifetime.

So how nice would it be to know that you've got money and that it's working to your advantage when you need it?

We're a nation still living with massive debt as a result of our overspending on credit, personal loans, high mortgage lending and now the new wave of "buy now pay later" mentality.

It's got to stop, people.

You've got to stop spending your hard-earned money on stuff that doesn't bring long-term happiness.

Too many times I've seen people rack up massive amounts of debt on stuff they can't resell or do anything with later. It's stuff that clutters their homes and adds no financial gain or value to their lives.

I just can't get my head around this overspending and how quickly some people lay blame on the banks or the government for putting them in a financial crisis.

YOU put yourself in the financial crisis, I'm sorry to say, with your overspending and your failure to put away any savings that can work for you when you most need it.

You can stop this madness once and for all if you're prepared to listen and do what I outline in this book.

So, if you're ready, read on. If you're not, I wish you the very best of luck.

Let's get you learning how to make money work to your advantage and not to your bank's or financial institution's benefit!

WHAT IS
FINANCIAL
MUSCLE?

—

O kay, to begin, I need to share with you what financial muscle is and what it means to have AWESOME financial muscle.

Financial muscle is wholly and solely about building strength in your money. It means having money behind you when times are tough, like during the COVID-19 pandemic.

When you don't have financial muscle, you're not living a full and happy life. That's because you're always worried about money and how you're going to survive when the bills arrive.

When someone has excellent financial muscle, it's because they've worked hard and made their money work equally as hard. They haven't squandered it or spent it on frivolous things. They've used the power of saving to their advantage. They don't rely on banks to keep them going. They rely on their own money and continue to build a safety net around them in case an unexpected situation arises.

Financial muscle is what you should strive for: the peace of mind that you've got money when and if you most need it.

You work hard, and you need to ensure that you make your money work just as hard during your working life. When you do this, you'll have something to show for it when your working years are over. You'll be able to sit back and enjoy retirement. You won't have to worry about living off an aged pension or about being able to go on holidays or spend money on the things you long to do during retirement.

So to recap: Having financial muscle is about taking the worry out of unexpected things that can, and often do, go wrong in life.

It's about knowing you've got it covered—you've got money behind you, and that gives you peace of mind.

How Do You Build
FINANCIAL MUSCLE?

—

Well, you start by taking a look at how you're managing your money.

This may seem obvious, but how many of you are checking your bank statement once a month, have a budget in place, or are being super mindful about how much you're spending?

I'm going to take a guess and say not a lot of you!

Why? Because if you did any one of the things I just mentioned, you wouldn't be having so much trouble staying out of debt.

When you're consciously aware of how much money is going out the door, especially when there's more going out than in, you tend to do something about it.

However, most of you just tap and go without a blink of an eye and use that piece of plastic without a thought about what you're spending.

This is how some of you get into a whole lot of trouble—debt trouble.

So today, your first real day of not spending more than you earn, I encourage you to go through your bank statement and look at what you've spent this month. See if any recurring spending habits are costing you your financial health!

When you go through your bank statement, take a good look at the stuff you're spending your hard-earned money on and ask yourself these two questions:

- Did you need half the things you bought?

- Could you have gone without them for a bit until all your debts were paid off?

Be honest with yourself.

When the shit hits the fan, as we experienced during the COVID-19 pandemic, do you wish you hadn't spent as much as you did over the last few months? Do you wish you'd put some money away instead, for the moments of uncertainty?

OH HELL YES YOU DO! And you wish you had been more careful with your money!

Okay. So you've made mistakes, overspent and haven't put away enough money for moments when things get uncomfortable, but you're here now. So let's explore how you can right the wrongs of the past and change your financial future.

Let me show you how you can start to build real financial muscle and get your money working once and for all for YOU!

WHAT IT LOOKS LIKE WHEN YOU
DON'T HAVE FINANCIAL MUSCLE

—

Before I get into teaching you how to build financial muscle, I would like you to take a look at this diagram:

This is what happens when you DON'T have Financial Muscle!

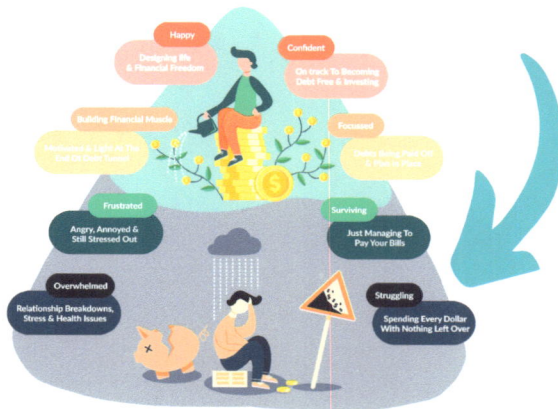

© Financial Management 101

You'll see at the bottom half of this illustration that when someone doesn't have financial muscle, they're putting themselves under constant stress.

You may be looking at this and experiencing some of the symptoms yourself and feeling very overwhelmed.

Generally, in this state a person's emotions are heightened and they may even be experiencing possible health issues along with relationship challenges.

Fights and arguments with loved ones go hand in hand, sadly, when people are under money stress.

When someone is struggling financially, they pretty much spend everything they earn and have nothing left at the end of payday. If they haven't quite hit rock bottom, they're frustrated and feel like they're only just surviving their financial situation.

In this stage, their frustrations are causing them to get angry quite quickly. They have very little patience and they feel pretty stressed out.

Most of the time when they're in survival mode, they only just manage to pay their bills and meet their financial commitments. It's a very worrying time for them.

I wouldn't like anyone to be in this position for a prolonged period of time, as it takes a toll on overall health.

WHAT IT LOOKS LIKE WHEN

YOU DO HAVE FINANCIAL MUSCLE

—

N ow, when you take a look at this illustration, you can see what a difference it can make in your life when you do have money working for you:

This is what happens when you DO have Financial Muscle!

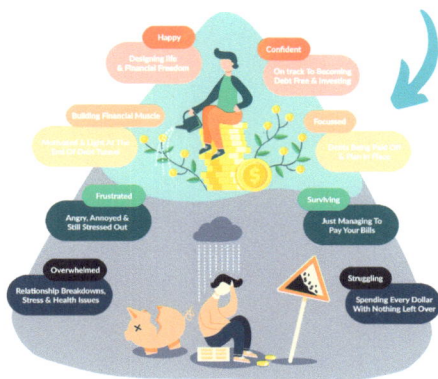

© Financial Management 101

You can see here that once a person manages to get out of the debt hole, life becomes a load more fun.

The individual is now starting to build financial muscle. Debts either are paid off or being paid off, which has relieved some of the financial strain.

When money is working for you, you're happier, more optimistic and confident about your life and future.

This is when you can get your money working smarter through wealth-building opportunities.

Can you imagine for a moment what it would be like to be debt-free and mortgage-free, and have some savings behind you?

Now imagine that you've cracked the whip on your money and it's hard at work in investing and growing while you start to think about your retirement options in a brighter frame of mind.

Life just got a whole lot easier.

This is the goal: To become debt-free and be in awesome financial health.

THE STEPS TOWARDS
FINANCIAL MUSCLE

T here are seven main steps to achieving awesome financial health. And each step is just as important as the others.

7 Steps To Building Financial Muscle

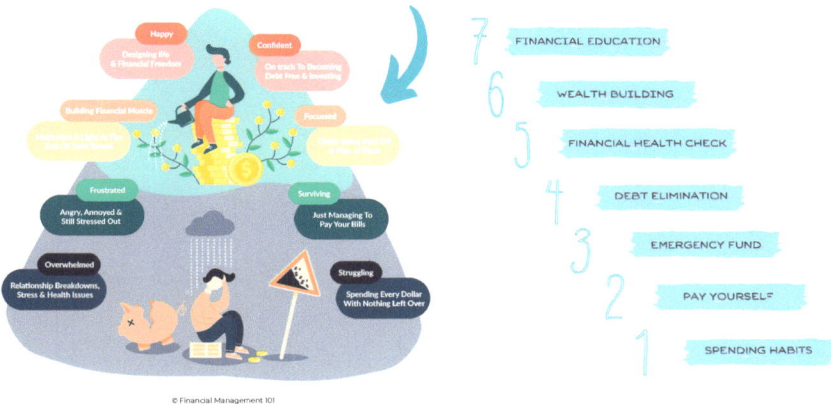

© Financial Management 101

I have put them in the order that I believe you need to follow to get back in the black and live a stress-free life, financially anyway.

If you follow the steps in this book, you'll be well on your way to building financial muscle and living a financially stress-free life.

So let's dig in, starting with the First Step - Your Spending Habits.

FIRST STEP
YOUR SPENDING HABITS

—

What are you spending your money on each and every payday?

Are you spending it on worthless things? Things that make you feel good in the short term but mean that when it comes to paying your bills or saving for your future, you haven't anything left?

My guess is that this is when you start to feel stressed out and your life becomes very overwhelming.

The quickest and easiest way to get a handle on what you're spending is to look at doing a budget.

For the first month, write down everything you spend. Then deduct that amount from what you earn.

More often than not, you've used credit to help get you out of a bind, but it's not working. You're getting further and further into debt, so your budget may put you in an unfavourable position.

Look, I agree with you, budgets aren't that fun. But they're the starting point to knowing where your money is going every payday and every month.

It can be a real eye-opener just to see how much you spend on non-essential items.

It's also an excellent way to see how much you're paying every month on debt, whether it's credit cards or, if you have one, your mortgage.

Making a budget is the first step to getting a handle on your money.

I recently had a client do this. She was amazed at how much she was spending on personal care, like hair, nails and makeup. She was buying expensive makeup because it made her feel good, but it ended up just sitting in her makeup case, not even being used.

I had another client get the shock of her life when she realised how much she was spending on lunches during the week.

When she did the numbers, she saw that the $60-plus dollars she spent on meals every month could've paid off her credit card in six months instead of the two years she had spent throwing away good money on interest payments.

So do your own numbers.

I've made it really easy with a spreadsheet that adds up as you go. All you have to do is spend about 15 minutes adding in what you've spent for the month.

Go through your bank and/or credit card statement. That will make it easier to do because it's itemised for you.

If you're interested in using my quick-and-easy budget/spending spreadsheet, click the link below and get instant access.

Karen's Budgeting Spreadsheet CLICK HERE.

Let me know how you go! Just drop me a note at team@financialmanagement101.com.au and don't forget to join my Facebook group at Official Karen G Community to share your progress.

I look forward to hearing about your results.

ACTION ITEM 1:

Go through your statements to determine what you're spending each month.

Download Karen's Budgeting Spreadsheet by heading over to www.financialmanagement101.com.au/resources to help you see where you're spending your money.

SECOND STEP

PAY YOURSELF FIRST

—

Next, once you've worked out if there's any surplus, you'll want to make some adjustments in your spending to put away a small percentage, around 10%, of what you earn into a savings account.

Now, 10% is not a lot of money. But you'll need to do this first at payday before you pay any bills or use some of your income on other expenditures.

Once you've put away 10%, or even $20 or $30, regularly into a savings account, then put this practice on autopilot. This is where every payday, money goes from your pay into this account automatically without you having to do a thing.

You want it set on autopilot so that you don't get tempted to spend it or stop it from going into your savings account. This way, it's kind of like a set-and-forget forced savings strategy.

Trust me: You won't miss it!

I guarantee that you'll start to think about your money a little differently when you see the balance growing your in saving account.

Something magical happens when you start to see your savings increase. You begin to feel more confident and less stressed, and this gives you a greater sense of security.

What you'll need to look for is an account that has no account-keeping fees and no exit fees.

Also, you DO NOT WANT an ATM card attached to this account. If you have a card for your savings, you may be tempted to withdraw from it when you feel you need some extra money.

BUT don't! This is you saving up for your future!

There are plenty of accounts out there, so do your homework to make sure you aren't slogged any fees.

Go to sites like finder.com and make the comparison.

My husband has an ING savings maximiser account. I use UBank, as I can link a Visa debit transaction card and get a higher rate of interest savings.

The Visa debit transaction card has no fees, including no foreign transaction fees when my monthly business subscriptions come out. This is one way I make money work to my advantage and not the bank's.

If you want to chat about your options or need some help understanding and comparing accounts, then pop into my Facebook group. I can help you with the terminology used for comparing each of the accounts on offer.

ACTION ITEM 2:

Research and find a savings account that you can put on autopilot for your "Pay Yourself First" savings account.

THIRD STEP
EMERGENCY FUND

—

In the third step, you've got to be strict with yourself: Open a second, separate savings account with the same features as your "Pay Yourself First" account.

You'll require an account that's hard to get access to, like your "Pay Yourself First" account. But this new account will be your emergency fund.

You'll need to get this account up to at least $2,000 as quickly as possible. Preferably, have about six to nine months of your income in this account as a safety net in case something happens - such as if you get sick or your work situation changes without notice.

This account will provide a safety net that takes the pressure off until you get back to work.

There are many ways to get this account up to $2,000.

One is to look around your home. Is there anything sitting around in your garage or shed that's gathering dust? Could you sell it to raise money for your emergency fund?

The emergency fund is the third most critical aspect to building financial muscle. That's because it takes the pressure off you and your money when those unexpected events arise, events like COVID-19.

The emergency fund is for precisely that: emergencies that make life very difficult if you can't work or don't have the means to get more money in the door quickly.

As I mentioned earlier, the emergency fund ideally needs to be at a balance that would allow you to pay your bills if you were to lose your job or be unable to work for six months. It's meant to support you until you can get back to working.

I cannot stress strongly enough how urgent it is for you to build up this account to a comfortable amount. If you do, it will alleviate any potential financial pressure that may arise.

ACTION ITEM 3:

Research an account for your emergency savings that has no upfront or ongoing fees.

Aim to have $2000 in this account ASAP

FOURTH STEP
DEBT ELIMINATION

▬

The primary stress for most people is their ever-increasing debt, whether it be from overspending on credit or the mortgage on their home.

I can promise you that when you finally become debt-free, life is going to be a whole lot more fun.

Things that used to stress you out will suddenly be gone, along with all the pressure of working at a job that you probably don't like. You now have the power and choice to look at whether you want to continue working there, or not.

If you're not working to pay down all your debts as fast as you can, you're just throwing away good money to the banking institutions that are funding your poor money habits. You're making them richer while you become poorer.

Map out who you owe and how much you owe. Then start with one debt at a time and pay it down until it's gone.

Once you've eliminated the first debt, use the money that you used to pay on the first debt to double up on the next debt.

If you need a helping hand to work out which debt to pay down first, download my debt reduction strategy. Head over to https://financialmanagement101.com.au/resources/ or follow the link HERE at Debt Repayment Strategy.

Before you download the debt elimination strategy, I want you to take a look at the consequences of throwing away good money to the banks by not paying down your debts as quickly as possible.

Take a look at the example in this illustration:

$10,000 @ 21%
= $175 p/m

24 years to pay off!!

Increasing to $30 p/wk = $305 p/m | 4 years to pay off

Increasing to $75 p/wk = $500 p/m | 2.1 years to pay off

You see here a person who has a $10,000 credit card balance. If they pay interest-only payments, it will take them 24 years to pay the debt off. PLUS, they'll sadly give thousands of dollars to the lending institution in interest because they didn't pay the debt off at the time the purchases were charged onto the credit card!

This is just one horrific example of throwing away good money because the balance isn't paid off in full every month!

However, by making extra payments to knock this card down to a $0 balance, they could pay this debt down in no time.

WHAT ARE YOU DOING WITH YOUR MONEY?

ACTION ITEM 4:

Download Karen's Debt Repayment Strategy and start working your way through which debt to pay off first.

Take action and begin to make extra repayments on your debt.

Fifth Step
FINANCIAL HEALTH CHECK

—

The next step in building financial muscle is to do a quick financial health check.

Quite simply, a financial health check will determine if there are any financial areas you need to work on or get more information about to get back on track and retire comfortably.

There's a five-minute Financial Health Check-Up that you can download HERE or head over to www.financialmanagement101.com.au/resources and get started.

The financial health check is going to cover four areas:

- **Your Financial Goals - Your Future :**

  Looks at whether you have financial goals in place and, if so, whether you feel you're on target to achieve them.

- **Cash Flow Management - Your Money** :

  Identifies how you feel about where your money is being spent and checks in with you to see if you could survive financially in the event of sickness, accident or job loss.

- **Debt Reduction - Stress-Free :**

  If you're a homeowner, identifies whether you're on track to paying your home loan down within the next ten years and are using mortgage reduction strategies to do this.

  If you're currently renting, determines whether owning your own home is an option you've been considering but just aren't sure how to go about making it a reality.

- **Retirement - Living the Life You Desire :**

  Evaluates whether you have plans in place for creating an income during retirement. Also determines if you know what investment options are available to you.

By identifying areas where you may need more help and support, a financial health check ensures you don't put yourself under any more stress.

FINANCIAL STRESS

Are you aware of how stress can affect your health?

Let's take a look at this illustration to see how stress can affect our body.

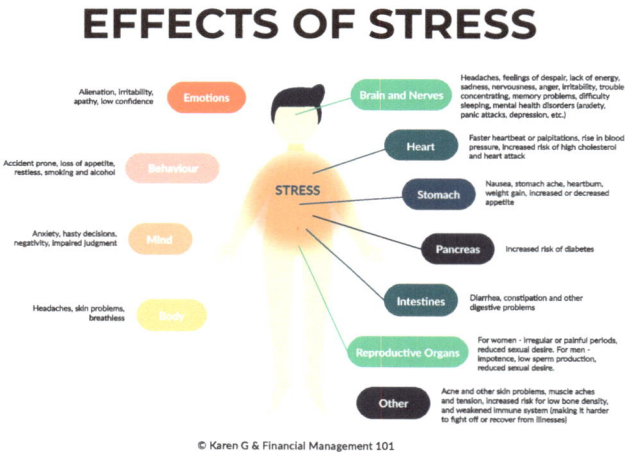

EFFECTS OF STRESS

Emotions — Alienation, irritability, apathy, low confidence

Behaviour — Accident prone, loss of appetite, restless, smoking and alcohol

Mind — Anxiety, hasty decisions, negativity, impaired judgment

Body — Headaches, skin problems, breathless

STRESS

Brain and Nerves — Headaches, feelings of despair, lack of energy, sadness, nervousness, anger, irritability, trouble concentrating, memory problems, difficulty sleeping, mental health disorders (anxiety, panic attacks, depression, etc.)

Heart — Faster heartbeat or palpitations, rise in blood pressure, increased risk of high cholesterol and heart attack

Stomach — Nausea, stomach ache, heartburn, weight gain, increased or decreased appetite

Pancreas — Increased risk of diabetes

Intestines — Diarrhea, constipation and other digestive problems

Reproductive Organs — For women - irregular or painful periods, reduced sexual desire. For men - impotence, low sperm production, reduced sexual desire.

Other — Acne and other skin problems, muscle aches and tension, increased risk for low bone density, and weakened immune system (making it harder to fight off or recover from illnesses)

© Karen G & Financial Management 101

Stress affects four main areas within your body.

The first is your emotions.

When your emotions are overloaded by stress, you become irritable, you may alienate yourself from others and your confidence drops.

When you're under stress, your behaviour changes and you may become accident prone, lose appetite, take up recreational drugs or alcohol, and/or start smoking.

Stress also affects your mind and mental well-being.

You may experience more anxiety, become negative or make impaired decisions and judgments where you otherwise wouldn't have done.

Stress can also affect you with stomach complaints either in the form of diarrhoea or heartburn.

In more severe cases, stress can even affect your heart. You may experience heart palpitations or worse still a heart attack.

So you can see it's more important than ever to take care of yourself and get your money in shape so that you can live a healthy, long life without added stress.

ACTION ITEM 5:

Download the FREE Financial Health Check-Up to see how you stack up.

Sixth Step
WEALTH-BUILDING

—

Y ou're saving money and you're paying off your debts. Now it's time to look at your wealth-building strategies.

Wealth-building is entirely different to just paying your bills and making ends meet. It's another series of steps that you take over the course of your working life. It involves planning your income and savings to provide yourself with a lifestyle when you've finished working and are ready to retire.

Wealth is having a group of assets that you'll enjoy in the years to come. These assets grow out of a series of wealth-building steps.

The steps to building wealth are highlighted in the following image:

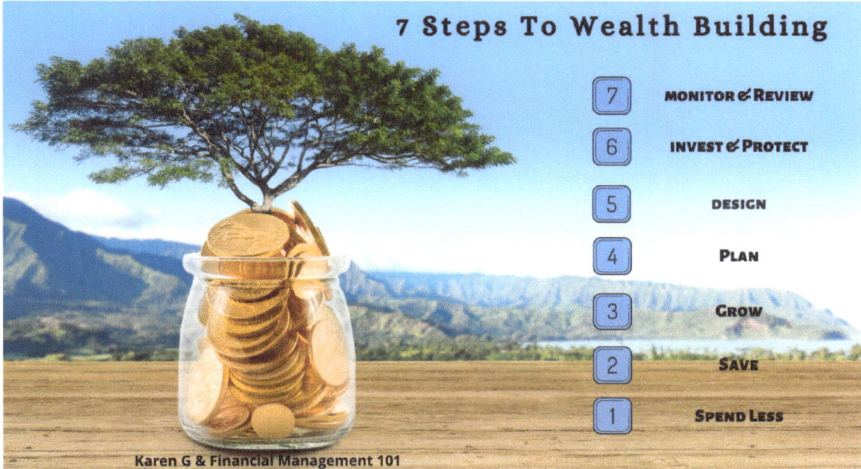

THE 7 STEPS TO WEALTH-BUILDING

- **Spend less than you earn-** This may seem obvious, but it's the key to having any real wealth and living a financially comfortable life.

- **Save-** As I've talked about in the previous chapters, save and put away as much as you can while you're still working.

- **Grow-** Save as much as you can while also growing your money in high-interest savings accounts until you have enough money to invest.

- **Plan-** Now is the time to work out how much money you'll need to live on when you retire and what your retirement lifestyle will look like. This is the time to map out what you plan to do during the years when you no longer have to work.

- **Design-** This is the stage when you look at your investment style. Your investment style is what you're comfortable investing in. It's personal, and it will determine whether you're a high-risk investor or prefer a more conservative style without too many risks.

- **Invest and Protect-** Now that you've decided on your investment style, this is where you look at the investment options available based on your design and risk tolerance.

- **Monitor and Review Regularly -** One of the most important steps is to review and regularly check that your investments are meeting your investment style and your projected income during retirement.

If you haven't already done so, find a financial planner who will assist you with the steps above to ensure you design a portfolio suitable to your investment needs.

A financial planner's job is also to monitor your investments and meet with you regularly to discuss how they're tracking. During your catch-ups, you address any concerns you may have so that you can tweak any issues before you're ready to retire.

Due to the scope and many facets briefly described above for wealth-building, I'm not going to go through each of the steps in detail. But I will talk about one area that I believe is VERY IMPORTANT. It's one you can work on now, while your money is growing.

That area is investing and protecting.

Let's talk about investing first.

INVESTING

SUPERANNUATION

Investing is about growing your money through superannuation and other investment options.

Superannuation (or "super" as it's called) is a way of saving for retirement. Essentially, your employer in Australia puts away a percentage of your salary into a fund of your choice. That money then invests until you retire.

It's a forced type of saving and a brilliant way to help those who are not good at saving.

It's one style of an investment option and will ensure you have some money at the end of your working life.

In Australia, money invested in your super fund is taxed at 15% on the income earned from the investments held within your super fund.

As a general rule of thumb, you can withdraw your super when you turn 65 (even if you haven't retired) when you reach preservation age and retire, or, under the transition to retirement rules, while continuing to work.

The question I'm often asked is, "How much super will I need at retirement?"

Well, the answer varies depending on many factors:

- The lifestyle you want when you retire.

- Any significant costs or expenses that need to be paid out at retirement, like paying off your mortgage, renovating your home and/or paying for medical expenses.

- Your life expectancy. Most people are living well into their 80s, so the amount you require will depend on when you plan on retiring and how long you're going to be here on Earth.

It's important to consider growing your super while working. You can do this by making extra payments on top of what your employer contributes on your behalf.

The smallest of amounts add up over time. It's worth chatting with a financial adviser if you don't know about maximising and growing your wealth-building opportunities through superannuation.

OTHER INVESTMENT OPTIONS

Other investment options for building wealth during your working years may consist of investing directly in shares, managed funds or property, to name a few.

These investments outside of superannuation are made with your after-tax dollars.

Finding the right investment option for you will depend on a few factors.

Firstly, you need to find investments that fit with your financial goals, investing timeframe and risk tolerance.

Next, you'll need to look at the type of investments that you're comfortable investing in. This is all done in the DESIGN PHASE, as in Step Five of the "7 Steps to Wealth Building."

There are several different investment styles, such as defensive, balanced and growth.

Defensive investments are considered lower risk. Investments into this category usually consist of 70% in cash and fixed interest investments, with the remaining 30% in shares and property.

Balanced investments are in the middle of the risk spectrum. The mix is around 50% into cash and fixed interest, with the other 50% into shares and property investments.

Growth, on the other hand, is considered a higher risk, but it offers a higher return compared to defensive investments. Growth investments are typically anywhere from 80/20 to 90/10 on the risk spectrum, with the higher percentage being in shares and property, and the lower percentage in cash and fixed-interest investments.

This is a general rule of thumb and a guide to the percentages that, when you invest, your money will be split into depending on your investment risk tolerances.

Your risk tolerance and where you're comfortable with investing is something you should discuss with your financial adviser.

In saying this, not everyone likes to invest in a mix of investments as described above. Some investors like to play the share market solely. Meanwhile, others enjoy investing purely in property, whether it be residential, industrial or within a managed property portfolio.

To find out your investment style, speak to your financial adviser.

If you're looking into wealth-building, I encourage you to seek a financial adviser who is qualified to provide advice on the assets and investment options that are best for you and your circumstances.

There are many financial advisers to choose from, so take the time to ensure you find one who has your best interest at the forefront of the advice they give.

ACTION ITEM 6 - PART 1:

Go through and find your superannuation fund and check it over to see:

- The balance of the fund

- What investment option you're in

- What fees you're being charged

- If there's a financial adviser attached to your account

PROTECTING

A WILL & ESTATE PLAN

Next, I want to talk about protecting your money. This is a crucial topic. Here I'll give you a good idea of how you need to be aware of protecting your wealth-building strategies.

Let's talk about why it's essential to have a will or an excellent estate plan in place.

A will and an estate plan ensure that your wishes at the end of your life are carried out and your assets are appropriately distributed.

A will is a legal document that states what you would like to have done with your assets when you die. It forms part of your estate plan.

An estate plan records exactly what you would like to happen with your assets upon death. It includes documents such as your will, a testamentary trust and superannuation assets. It may also contain powers of attorney or other such documents that allow you to appoint someone to act on your behalf if you're unable to make decisions.

So, as you can see from the brief descriptions above, it's extremely important to make sure you're protecting what you've worked long and hard to build.

If you die without making a will, it means you die "intestate." This can cause a great deal of heartache and headache for your loved ones left behind.

When a person dies intestate, the Supreme or highest Court of your state will appoint an administrator.

The administrator's job is to arrange the funeral and distribute any leftover assets after paying any debts and taxes.

Sometimes there are fees associated with an administrator taking care of your assets. That means your loved ones may not receive the full inheritance you had planned on leaving them.

So, make it your priority today to ensure you have a current will—because nobody knows when their time is up.

ACTION ITEM 6 - PART 2:

Make sure you have a valid will. If not, go get one done ASAP.

SEVENTH STEP
FINANCIAL EDUCATION & SUPPORT

—

And last but not least, the seventh step to building financial muscle is getting ongoing financial education and support.

Think of sporting teams, which use coaches to help guide them to greatness and victory. Financial education combined with financial coaching is exactly the same.

Obtaining financial education while feeling supported during your financial journey ensures that you move out from the herd mentality and become debt-free and happy.

As an experienced financial coach, I know how to help, guide and coach you in matters relating to your financial well-being.

One of the many strategies I can assist you in is following the "7 Steps to Building Financial Muscle."

Working with me will make the difference between living with poverty or above the poverty line, happy and stress-free.

It's not all about the numbers; it's also about ensuring that you stay mentally healthy while you get into a financial position you can be proud of and happy with.

If you've read this far and you've followed the steps outlined above, then congratulations! You're committed to living a financially comfortable life.

Why not continue with your financial education by working with me every month?

I offer several free and also paid options. However, the most powerful is getting into my MONTHLY COACHING program.

This is one of the most inexpensive and effective ways you can move into achieving awesome financial health. It's incredibly supportive and an excellent way to build a financially stress-free life.

Check out more on the monthly coaching program in the LEARNING HUB for more details, see the resources section at the end of the book.

ACTION ITEM 7:

Check out the Learning Hub and Karen's financial coaching program by heading over to http://www.financialmanagement101.com.au/courses.

Reach out to me if you have any questions, at karen@financialmanagement101.com.au

Ultimately, financial muscle is about taking the worry out of unexpected things that can, and often do, go wrong.

It's about knowing you've got it covered—you have money behind you, and that gives you peace of mind.

It's been an absolute pleasure having you read my book. I look forward to working with you if not now, soon.

So here's to your financial health, wealth and happiness.

RESOURCES

———

To help you further expand your financial knowledge and succeed in your journey to a financially strong and stress-free life, I'll leave you with some links to the resources I have shared in this book.

Wherever you may be in that financial journey, I hope you join me in gaining more financial education. Just check out the resources I make available for you.

Take care. I wish you all the financial health, wealth and happiness in the world.

FREE Course:	How To Build Financial Muscle www.howtobuildfinancialmuscle.com
Facebook Group:	Official Karen G Community www.facebook.com/groups/officialkareng
Monthly Coaching:	Group Coaching https://financialmanagement101.com.au/courses
Meet Karen:	Karen's Experience www.financialmanagement101.com.au/meetkaren
Website:	Financial Management 101 https://financialmanagement101.com.au
Online Learning:	Learning Hub www.learninghub.financialmanagement101.com
Podcasts:	Easy Listening www.financialmanagement101.com.au/category/podcast

MEET THE
AUTHOR

—

Karen G, otherwise known as Karen Giglia Adams, started her career in financial services back in 1986.

She built up an extensive wealth of knowledge over those 30+ years. You can read more on Karen's experience and achievements on her website, under the "Meet Karen" section.

Karen's passion is, without a doubt, helping people realise their full potential in life, whether it be in their financial or emotional journey.

One of the areas that Karen is dedicated to is teaching, educating and empowering people with the knowledge to take back control of their money so they can live happier and less stressed lives.

She's known around the world as the person to call when you want to learn how to build financial muscle.